The Janna Years

A play

Gillian Plowman

Samuel French - London
New York - Toronto - Hollywood

© 1991 GILLIAN PLOWMAN

Rights of Performance by Amateurs are controlled by Samuel French Ltd, 52 Fitzroy Street, London W1P 6JR, and they, or their authorized agents, issue licences to amateurs on payment of a fee. **It is an infringement of the Copyright to give any performance or public reading of the play before the fee has been paid and the licence issued.**

The Royalty Fee indicated below is subject to contract and subject to variation at the sole discretion of Samuel French Ltd.

> Basic fee for each and every
> performance by amateurs   Code D
> in the British Isles

The Professional Rights in this play are controlled by MICHAEL IMISON PLAYWRIGHTS LIMITED, 28 ALMEIDA STREET, LONDON N1 1TD.

The publication of this play does not imply that it is necessarily available for performance by amateurs or professionals, either in the British Isles or Overseas. Amateurs and professionals considering a production are strongly advised in their own interests to apply to appropriate agents for consent before starting rehearsals or booking a theatre or hall.

ISBN 0 573 12125 7

Please see page iv for further copyright information.

THE JANNA YEARS

First presented by the Flat Four Players with the following cast:

Abe	David Flint
Fleur	Lorna Fletcher
Holly	Karrie Stark
Chas	Derek Benfield
Ruby	Jenny Mummery

CHARACTERS

Abe, in his forties, divorced
Fleur, single, twenties
Holly, single, late twenties, plump
Chas, northerner, between thirty and forty
Ruby, landlady, late forties

The action takes place in the communal room of Ruby's boarding-house

Time – the present

Other plays by Gillian Plowman
published by Samuel French Ltd

Cecily
David's Birthday
Me and My Friend
Tippers
Two Summers

THE JANNA YEARS

The communal room at Ruby's boarding-house

There is a winged chair in the centre of the room with a standard lamp on the right hand side of it and a wastepaper bin on the left. The room is in darkness apart from the lamp

Abraham (Abe) is sitting in the chair with a box on his lap. He is reading a letter by the light of the lamp

Child's Voice (*off*) Dear Daddy, I wish you hadn't gone away. I don't understand why Mummy and I can't come too. I really don't mind leaving all my friends here—I know I said I did, but I don't. Is it my fault, Daddy? I don't think you should be divorced, because I love you both . . . Janna.

The voice fades and Abe puts the letter back in the box

Pause. The Lights come up

Fleur comes in with a small armchair which she puts facing Abe's. She then brings a low easel, paints, brushes and a half-finished, unique to Fleur, portrait of Abe. She brings a tall green plant and places it beside Abe's chair. She spends some time arranging it, then sits down with satisfaction

Fleur Hallo, Abe.
Abe Hallo, Fleur.
Fleur Reading all your letters again?
Abe 'Fraid so.
Fleur I'll write you one one day.
Abe Will you?
Fleur When we live in different places. Will you keep them in a bundle?
Abe Of course. (*He moves into position*) OK?

Fleur indicates for him to move to the right position with her hands

Fleur That's fine. (*Pause*) Have you had any interesting complaints today?
Abe One lady. She'd bought some hair tongs, you know.

Fleur For making curly hair.

Abe She overdid it. She wanted an abandoned style for a special weekend, she said, so she dyed it red, then curled it up one way, then the other, then it fell out.

Fleur giggles

Fleur (*whispering*) It wasn't Ruby, was it?

Abe (*whispering*) That would have been against the rules. (*In his normal voice*) She sent a photo.

Fleur Of her abandoned weekend?

Abe Of her head.

Fleur Have you got it?

Abe It's in my office.

Fleur You've got this lady's head in your office? (*She starts to giggle*)

Abe Well, I am Head of Complaints!

Fleur splutters

She looks like one of your paintings.

Fleur What do you mean?

Abe Incredibly unique.

Fleur Will you bring it to show me tomorrow?

Abe Tomorrow's Saturday.

Fleur Oh yes. Will you sit for me? I could finish this!

Abe It's my weekend to see Janna.

Fleur Oh. (*Pause*) I think Holly wants me to go to a jumble-sale anyway.

Abe That's nice.

Fleur Is she coming tonight?

Abe I'm trying not to get ready too soon.

Fleur Trying not to get excited. I know.

Abe You're a wise thing.

Fleur Am I? Is that the same as being clever?

Abe It needn't be.

Fleur It's the Scouts and Guides jumble-sale. They've combined. They're raising money for a tent. They're going to share it.

Abe They really have combined then.

Fleur Oh no! They're both going to use it for camp, but they're not going at the same time. Oh, Abe. (*She giggles*) I was a Girl Guide.

Abe Were you?

Fleur For six months. When I was with the foster mother in Post Office Road. But when I moved to the new foster mother in North Road, it was too far to go. I never went to camp.

Abe Didn't you?

Fleur I wish I had. I've never been to the country.

Abe It's not far away.

Fleur I know. I am going.

Abe Fleur? Did you miss not having a father?

Fleur I had quite a few. They're not very interested in children, though, are they, fathers? Well, you are, I know, but you can't do that much about it, can you?

Abe I'd better grab the bathroom ... (*He rises*)

Fleur wants him to stay

Fleur I just want to do this bit. What else you done today?

Abe I've thought a lot.

Fleur I wish I could. I try to—quite a bit, but when I think about whether I've thought about anything ... I can't think what I've thought about.

Abe It doesn't matter. It gives you a headache.

Fleur Poor Abe. Were you thinking about Janna? (*She puts some colour on the painting*) There. That's a headache. And what're you going to do this weekend?

Abe And how much I love her.

Chas enters, looking very dirty, in a boiler suit. He carries a bunch of flowers and a bag from the off-licence, with bottles in

Chas 'Evening all. Bags I the bath.

Abe I was just going.

Chas I need it. Got a date. Met this lovely little black-eyed Susie. Little bit of chat, bunch of flowers, bottle of plonk ... who knows, I may not be back tonight.

Fleur You've got a wife in ... up there, Chas.

Chas Can't afford to get back ... up there ... every weekend, flower. She doesn't want me to be miserable. Unless you want to cheer me up.

Abe Lay off, Chas.

Chas Oops, sorry. Cutting in, am I?

Fleur (*wagging her finger at him reprimandingly*) We're all good
   friends here.
Chas Pity.
Fleur Ruby says you should wash before you come home.
Chas I didn't want to miss the transport, flower.
Fleur Fleur. It's French.
Chas Sexy lot, the French.

   Chas goes to his room

Fleur Go on, quick, get your things!
Abe I thought you wanted me to sit.
Fleur You'll never get clean after he's been in there. Him and his
   black bathroom rings. I can carry on on my own for a bit. I've
   done the headache.

   Abe goes to his room

*Fleur goes to stand in front of the entrance to the bathroom, which
she does with her arms outstretched*

   *Holly emerges from her room in a long shirt, yawning. She finds
   the way to the bathroom barred*

Holly I need a wee.
Fleur You'll have to go down on the landing. Abe's going to have
   a bath.
Holly I'll only be a minute.

   *Chas and Abe come out of their rooms with towels and wash kits
   at the same time*

Holly Fleur!
Fleur No! (*She brings her fists up like a boxer*)
Holly Well, I'm not that desperate for a wee. I'll go down on the
   landing.

   Holly goes out of the main entrance

Chas What's it to be? Toss of a coin or pistols at dawn.
Abe Toss for it.
Chas Here you are then, flower, you can do it.

*He holds out a coin and Fleur comes to get it. She tosses it as Chas
moves casually towards the bathroom*

Fleur What do you want, Abe?
Abe Heads.
Fleur Heads it is. Abe has the bathroom.

But Chas has gone in and shut the door

Fleur flies into a rage

Fleur That's not fair. Come out of there. You cheating, lying
   sod . . .
Abe Fleur! It's all right . . .
Fleur You filthy, greasy bugger. It was heads! Abe had heads! You
   didn't have heads! You had tails! Fish tails, slimy tails . . . It's
   against the rules to leave black rings round the bath!

*During all this, Ruby enters. A well-groomed, middle-aged lady
   who loves to live up to her name, she has red hair and red clothes*

Ruby Fleur!
Fleur It's not fair!

*Fleur flings herself into her chair and shakes with anger. She mixes
her paint with venom and splashes it on to the canvas*

Ruby I told your social worker, dear, that if you have any more
   fits, he'll have to find you somewhere else to live. It's a good job
   I don't keep any furniture in this room.
Abe It wasn't her fault. Chas and I were arguing over the
   bathroom.
Fleur I've put my anger on to his picture now!

Holly enters

Abe I don't mind.
Ruby What the hell do you think you're doing, going outside
   undressed like that?
Holly I'm back now.
Ruby You know the rules. To be in this room, you have to be
   properly dressed.

Fleur flings herself out of her chair, still shaking with anger

Fleur She's got her knickers on! One of my mothers used to say
   you're always properly dressed if you've got your knickers on.
Holly I'm sorry, Ruby, I was half asleep.

Ruby She'll have to go, you know.

Holly ⎫ (*together*) ⎧ Over my dead body!

Fleur ⎭   ⎩ Who'll have to go?

Holly (*quickly*) Me, I expect.

Ruby (*to Holly*) You know who I mean. (*To Fleur*) You're not normal, you're not.

Holly She's artistic.

Ruby And you've been in all day. This is bed and breakfast and an evening meal.

Holly I was doing the bed bit.

Ruby You're not supposed to be here unless I know about it.

Holly How did you know about it?

Ruby You snore.

Holly How soul-destroying.

Abe Aren't you well, Holly?

Holly Furious, actually.

Fleur I get that.

Holly I'm the only girl on our sales team; I helped them get this latest contract, and they decide to sign it over a stag lunch.

Abe Do you want your chair?

Holly Yes please. A strip lunch.

Abe goes to get Holly's easy chair from her room

Fleur They took their clothes off?

Holly No, some girls did. Or a girl did. If that's the only way some stupid girl can earn a living, I feel sorry for her.

Fleur I do. Do you want me to get your robe?

Holly Yes please.

Ruby Oh, thank God.

Fleur goes to Holly's room passing:

Abe as he enters with Holly's chair

Holly I did a lot of research. Some of those papers were mine.

Abe Here you are.

Holly So I said, "I'm not coming in if I'm not going out," so they gave me the day off, which I didn't want, but it goes against the grain to hold the fort whilst they're all lunching on expenses, so I didn't go in and now I don't know what's going on.

Ruby Well, a girl stripping isn't much going on.

Abe They wouldn't have got much done with a girl stripping.

Fleur brings in Holly's very ostentatious robe

Holly I bet one of those ... men ... will get the credit for my work. Agh!

Fleur Do you want me to jump up and down for you?

Ruby It was ever thus.

Holly No. I've given in my notice.

Ruby The first time I got married, I walked down the aisle on my father's arm, and the vicar said, "Who giveth this woman?" and my father said proudly, because I looked lovely, "I do". And my mother sat crying in the front row, and I thought, hang on. She was the one who went through a rotten rationed nine months, she was the one who washed and cleaned and sewed my clothes, nursed me through measles, chicken pox, you name it, I had it, due to the colour of my hair, I think, and dried eggs; combed my hair with a fine toothcomb because other children had fleas, made me birthday cakes, bought my first pair of nylons. Gave me my first perm when I was thirteen. Went disastrously wrong but she provided me with sick notes till it grew out. She did all that, and here was him taking all the credit. "Here you are, mate, and lovely she is." You want to remember that, Abe, when you march your little girl down the aisle. Your wife's done all the work. I'm going to get the rent book. What do you mean, you've given in your notice? This is not a doss house. Everybody goes out to work here.

Holly Don't talk to me about work. I've worked my ass off doing two jobs in order to save. Well now I'm going to stick to modelling. They've asked me to do a lot more.

Ruby With your figure?

Holly There are more people my size, than there are stick and skinny. The Plump and Pretty Model Agency is where it's all happening.

Abe Ruby, could my daughter come here this weekend?

Ruby No children.

Abe She's fifteen.

Holly Why can't he bring her here? It's his home. Such as it is.

Ruby It clearly states in the rules. He knew that when he moved in.

Ruby goes out

Abe, Fleur and Holly sit in their chairs

Abe I booked the *Railway Hotel* this weekend, but I'm sure Janna hates it. There's nothing to do. Her mother says she doesn't want to come any more.

Fleur 'Course she does. That's just her mother saying that. They don't know what you really think.

Abe She's too old for zoos and parks. Films she likes, but she's always seen whatever's on. She loves shopping. That's why I thought, if we saved the hotel bill, we'd have more to go shopping with.

Fleur She could come to the jumble sale. Are we going Holly?

Abe Janna doesn't like jumble sales. She has everything new. Her mother insists, and I promised. It's only fair.

Holly What did you do, Abraham, to get yourself in such a mess?

Pause

Abe I fell in love with a beautiful woman. And I told my wife.

Pause. They look at him expectantly. Abe is lost in the past

Holly You had an affair.

Fleur What happened to the beautiful woman?

Abe She went to Doncaster by car.

Holly What?

Fleur I've never been in love, Abie. Tell me what it's like.

Abe I was in a train, travelling home after a business meeting, and she was in the same compartment. I tried hard not to but I couldn't help looking at her. Brown eyes, and a soft, sad mouth and such fine skin that I wanted to touch it. She was very smart—in a black suit with a brooch in the shape of a butterfly on one lapel. And she wore her hair coiled around the back of her head, and a black hat with a tiny veil. The first time she caught my eye, she smiled at me. And I fell in love.

Fleur Oh, Abe.

Holly You don't fall in love because somebody smiles at you.

Abe You do, Holly. Oh, you do.

Pause

Fleur I guess ... not many people smile at me then.

Abe When the train stopped, we were the only two in the carriage. She wasn't frightened. We'd started talking by then. It was an accident. We were stopped for four hours. Together for four hours. It got cold, and we sat together to keep warm. I held her. Her name was Elizabeth.

Fleur Did you kiss?

Abe No.

Holly What did you talk about?

Abe Everything. Our lives, our childhoods, our families. Bluebells, the cold war, history, the Bahamas. She'd lived in the Bahamas. Once or twice, the train lurched, and we held each other so tight. I wanted her forever.

Holly And you told your wife that?

Abe I dreamt it was possible.

Fleur Did you see Elizabeth again?

Abe They came and took us off the train—we had to walk across a field. We held hands. But when we reached the road, there were so many people ... there was a man who called out "Elizabeth, thank God", and he just picked her up and put her into a car. No, I never saw her again. I've nothing to offer her anyway.

Holly You got divorced over a meeting in a train?

Abe My wife couldn't forgive me.

Holly But you didn't do anything!

Abe I stopped loving her. She asked me to leave.

Holly And you send her all your money.

Abe Yes, of course. She doesn't deserve not to be loved.

Holly So she's got a beautiful house?

Abe Yes.

Holly Clothes. Car?

Abe nods

Does she work?

Abe She has to look after Janna.

Holly And you live in a dump like this. You're bonkers.

Abe You live here.

Holly Whilst I save up to buy me own place.

Fleur I know an Elizabeth. The lady I clean on Thursdays. Her wardrobe's got a black suit in it. And I'm sure she's got a black hat with a veil. Perhaps it's her. Shall I ask her?

Abe ⎫
Holly ⎬ (*together*)   No.

Fleur gets up and goes to the bathroom entrance

Fleur Boilerman! How long you going to be?
Chas (*off*) Getting the grime out of me bits.
Abe I'll have a bath at the *Railway Hotel*, if there's any hot water. Better iron a shirt. Though I don't want to put a clean shirt on a dirty body.
Holly Action stations. Go and get your shirt. Fleur go and get the ironing board. Both of you give me your rent and I'll stop Madame coming back in.
Fleur She's already got my Giro. She never lets me open it, says it's for her anyway.

Fleur exits for the ironing-board

Abe There's mine.

Abe goes to get his shirt

Holly takes the rent and goes out of the main entrance

Fleur brings the ironing board and iron in

Abe brings in his ironing

Holly comes back with a washing up bowl

Holly I've switched the kettle on. Take your clothes off.
Abe What!
Holly (*to Fleur*) Table.

Fleur goes out and returns with a table

Abe Nobody is allowed in this room unless properly dressed.
Holly Properly dressed for washing is bare.
Abe Oh no . . .
Holly (*chanting*) Pick up de bowl . . .

Holly and Fleur take appropriate actions during the next dialogue

Fleur De bowl, de bowl . . .
Holly And put it on the table . . .
Fleur Table, table . . .
Holly Take off de shirt . . .
Fleur De shirt, de shirt.

Holly And trousers if you're able ...
Fleur Able, able ...
Abe I'll do it!
Holly I'll go and get the kettle ...
Fleur Kettle, kettle ...

Holly goes out

Abe puts a towel round his waist and takes off his trousers

Holly returns with the kettle

Holly Filled with nice hot water ...
Fleur Water, water ...
Holly Clean and smelling sweetly ...
Fleur Sweetly, sweetly ...
Holly To go and meet your daughter ...
Fleur Daughter, daughter ...
Abe I used to bathe Janna on the table. In front of the fire. Dress her and wrap her up warmly, and read her a story.

He pauses as he rubs the soap on to the flannel, and Holly takes it off him and washes his back. Fleur irons the shirt

I was lucky, I know. She was often naughty all day for my wife, but when we had our bedtime story, she was as good as gold. Best part of the day for me.
Fleur Can she read on her own now?
Abe She could read by the time she was four—very clever little thing. I taught her. But she indulged me, really. She was still letting me read to her right up until ... I had to leave. She was eleven then.

Holly carries on washing Abe

Fleur You had eleven Janna years.
Abe Janna years?
Fleur It's how I divide up my life. I had four baby years—before I remember anything—three Shirley years, two Doreen years, two Sam'n'Mary years and so on, you see, and now I'm in the Ruby years, 'cos I'm living in her house.

Pause

You could read to me.

Holly Don't be silly, Fleur. You don't like stories. You never
    read.

Pause

Fleur I can't.

Pause

Holly You can't read? Why not.
Fleur Nobody taught me.
Abe You went to school, didn't you?
Fleur Lots. I think I did learn, but I forgot it. It doesn't matter,
    though. I listen to the radio whilst I'm doing me jobs, and I put
    the television on when I'm doing those rooms, so I keep up with
    the news, and I know about gardening. I wish there was a
    garden here. I like it when they read stories.

Holly and Abe have paused mid-wash whilst listening to Fleur

Chas comes in from the bathroom with just a towel round his waist

Chas Stop! Stop! The bathroom's free now. Or I could go and
    occupy it again for a small fee. Lucky devil, Abe. How do I get
    my back scrubbed?
Holly No way.
Chas I can assure you he's got nothing that I haven't.
Holly God, men.
Chas Don't you like them?
Holly Not when they're brash and obvious.
Chas Like Chas.
Holly Correct.
Chas Sub-telty, Chas.

Chas goes into his room

Abe puts one foot in the bowl to wash it

*Chas pushes his easy chair back into the room, upon which is a pile
of ironing, which he gives to Fleur*

I've got some ironing, flower, if you're in the mood.
Holly That's not subtle.
Chas No, that's masterful. Still not impressed, huh?
Fleur I'm only doing this because you stole the bathroom.

Chas And because he has got something I haven't.
Holly (*to Abe*) Your towel's slipping.
Chas And we're about to find out what.

Holly holds the towel up whilst Abe does his foot. Fleur plonks Chas's ironing on his head and threatens him with the iron

  Ruby enters. There is silence

Ruby I've come for your rent. (*She holds out her hand to Chas*)
Chas I thought you'd come for the orgy.

Abe is starting to lose his balance

Ruby I will not be mocked. When I found myself, on my own, with an apartment that seemed, in this homeless day and age, to lend itself to the furtherance of my altruistic nature, I chose to help people to help themselves. At a very reasonable rent. One unfortunate on social security . . .
Fleur I do my jobs . . .
Ruby But the Inland Revenue doesn't know about that, dear, and it helps pay the rent. One single woman battling to get a mortgage in these days of so-called equality and rocketing interest rates. One divorcee crippled with maintenance payments, and one working-class hero trying to bridge the north south divide. I am the port in your life's storm, and the least you can bloody do is to obey the house rules, and put some clothes on!

Abe loses his balance and clutches at the nearest person—Ruby—as they fall to the ground. There is a horrible silence

Holly You all right, Ruby?

Ruby gets unsteadily to her feet

Ruby I lived for ten years with a man who beat me every Friday night. I just . . . remembered what it felt like.
Abe I'm so sorry . . .

Ruby starts to walk out

Chas Ruby!

Ruby turns. Chas goes into his room and comes out with the bunch of flowers

I brought them for you. For my first week as your lodger.

Ruby takes the flowers without a word and drops them in the wastepaper bin

    She goes out

Chas What is it about you, Chas? Oh well, we'll see how Susie likes them.

    He retrieves the flowers and goes out to his room

Abe I haven't bought anything for Janna

Fleur She can have my painting of you. When it's finished.

    Pause

Holly Take this. (*She takes off her robe*)

Fleur That's her *robe*, Abe. She'll like Holly's robe.

Holly It's new. The agency let me keep it after my last job. And clean. I'll just iron the belt. You can tell her it's off a real, live model. (*She irons the belt*)

Abe If she doesn't like it, I'll bring it back.

Fleur She'll like it. It's a present from you.

Abe Thank you.

    Abe takes the robe, picks up his washing things and goes to his room

    Holly picks up the bowl and goes out of the main entrance

    Fleur wipes her paint brushes on a rag and goes out

    Ruby comes back in. She has a cardigan pulled round her. She goes to the wastepaper bin and finds one flower is left there. She picks it up and looks at Chas's door. She goes to knock, then changes her mind. She switches off the lamp

The Lights snap off

    Ruby goes out in the Black-out

The Lights come up brightly. It is daytime the next day—Saturday

    There is a lively chattering as Fleur and Holly come in with their carrier bags full of jumble-sale purchases

Fleur All of this for four pounds thirty! Aren't people mad at jumble sales? I found ... (*she searches through till she finds the garment*) this! on the floor and had to get six pairs of feet off it before I could pick it up. Shall I try it on? (*She removes her clothes as she speaks and puts on the garment, probably a dress*) Is it nice?

Holly It is actually. Needs a wash, but it suits you. If we turn this into a shawlly thing (*she picks up a floral garment with a lot of skirt*) and drape it round, it'll look great.

Fleur You're clever, Holly.

Holly You pick up these tips, modelling.

Fleur I hope they made enough for a tent.

Holly Hey! Talking of tents, what about this? (*She puts on a voluminous dress*)

Holly and Fleur sing and dance as they put on the clothes. They turn US, when the door opens and they stop singing

> *Abe comes in. He holds his little case and a present, wrapped up. He gives this to Holly*

Abe Open it!

Holly looks at Fleur and opens it. It is the robe

> She didn't come.

Fleur Abie.

Abe goes to his chair

Abe She wasn't on the train. I waited for the next one. And the next. It was getting late. I was worried.

Holly and Fleur remove the jumble-sale clothes and, as and when, sit in their chairs either side of Abe

> I phoned my wife. There was no reply. I didn't know what to do. I went back to the *Railway Hotel*. No message. Back to the station. Back to the phone ... not on the last train. Such awful things can happen to women on trains ...

Pause

> I phoned the police. In Colchester. Asked them to go to the house.

Pause

Fleur Did they go?
Abe It was empty. They went to the neighbours.

Pause

Holly What did they say?
Abe They thought that my wife and Janna ... had gone away for
the weekend. I phoned her mother, and her sister—all the
family. No-one knows where they are, and her mother said it
was nothing to do with me anyway.
Holly Bloody cheek.
Abe I phoned the police again, and they said it was nothing to do
with them anymore. People are allowed to go away for the
weekend. British Rail said they couldn't help it if she wasn't on
one of their trains, and the *Railway Hotel* said I had to pay for
the rooms.

Chas enters with a crumpled look and crumpled flowers

I didn't sleep all night ...
Chas Neither did I. Nudge nudge, wink wink ...

Chas walks across and into his room

Abe I'll go and ring again.
Holly Perhaps Ruby would let you use her phone, under the
circumstances.
Abe I'll go and ask her.

Abe goes out

Chas comes in

Chas OK. I'm going to try honesty. It's very interesting on a
balcony six storeys up *all* night, with a slight frost for company.
(*He holds out the weary flowers at arms length*)
Holly Who are they for now?
Chas Cheer the place up, won't they?
Fleur Holly! I knew it was a good idea!

*Fleur rummages around in more jumble-sale bags and finds a chipped
vase. She holds it out and Chas puts the flowers in*

I'll get some water.

She hands the vase to Holly and goes out

Chas There were sixteen railings, one broken. Four chipped bricks, seventeen cracks in the concrete—I made a road system out of them—great big cracks were the motorways, little thread cracks were B roads. I used dead leaves for vehicles. Mine was a Porsche. Got blown over the side.

Holly You weren't sub-tel enough.

Chas Oh, she wanted the obvious ...

Holly But her husband came home. Did he? Ah! (*She shrieks with mirth*)

Chas Seconds after we got there. What a dim woman. I could have crept out whilst they were asleep, but she locked the balcony door. (*Pause*) It was two hours and thirty-nine minutes exactly between the last drunk and the first postman. Four ambulances passed, three police cars and a fire engine. Not all at the same time, and not quietly. What the hell goes on all night? Bloody street lamp was on all the time. Waste of electricity, I thought. Waste of tax-payers' money. A cat shrieked at me from across the way, and, believe it or not, I saw a fox rooting in the dustbins. A fox! In a high-rise housing estate!

Holly Which you wouldn't have seen without the street lamp. Urban nature study. It's an ill wind.

Chas They didn't surface till lunchtime. I got some funny looks from the neighbours. Had to pretend I was mending the railings, and that I was deaf.

Holly Deaf?

Chas They kept wanting to know when I was going to do theirs.

Holly How did you escape?

Chas He went out after lunch ...

Holly Not out on to the balcony?

Chas And she let me in.

Holly Oh good.

Chas Then she wanted me to stay! Can you believe that?

Holly Not really. I don't know what she was thinking of in the first place.

Chas Oh thanks, Prickles.

Holly What if it was your wife?

Chas What was?

Holly Inviting men in for the night whilst you're down here making an honest bob.

Chas My wife wouldn't do that.

Holly Why not?

Chas Because I love her.

Holly strokes her chin and looks at him contemplatively

What?

Holly (*slowly as to a child*) If you love your wife, why aren't you faithful to her?

Chas I am. I sat on a balcony all night.

Holly (*quickly to catch him out*) If you love your wife, why did you try to have sex with somebody else?

Chas If you were a man, you'd understand!

Fleur enters with the kettle of water, which she pours into the vase

Chas goes to his room and returns with the bottles of wine and gets out his pocket knife, which has a corkscrew on it

Holly It looks like you went out and came back with everything intact!

Chas opens the wine

Fleur What would you understand, Holly?

Holly Why men need sex.

Fleur How old are you?

Holly Old enough to know why men need sex, I suppose.

Chas Better to have it and not need it than need it and not have it.

Holly My mother used to say that about my mackintosh.

Chas Want a drink?

Holly You need a hobby.

Holly goes out through the main entrance

Chas I've got one. Sex is good for recreation as well as procreation.

Fleur So is swimming.

Chas looks at her

It's good exercise.

Chas You're not allowed to do *it* in the swimming pools I know.

Fleur Mine's painting. Would you like me to do you next?

Chas Can't sit still long enough, flower.

Holly comes back with four white tea cups

Chas pours wine into them

  Abe comes in

Abe Still no reply.
Fleur Did Ruby let you ring?
Abe Yes.
Fleur Good old Rube.
Holly It didn't cost her anything.
Fleur It would have done if there'd been a reply. (*She stops short and looks at Abe*)
Holly Have a cup of wine, Abie, we're celebrating.
Abe What?
Holly Chas's fidelity.
Chas To my fidelity!

They all drink

Fleur Well done, Chas.
Chas Thank you. Thank you all very much. D'you know, I'm beginning to feel really good about this.
Holly It's not everybody who could . . . not do it, the way you've not done it.
Fleur Abe, I'm sorry . . .
Abe Congratulations, Chas.
Chas It was nothing, honestly. I'm sure you could have not done it just as well. (*He pours more drinks*)
Abe No I couldn't. I haven't anyone to not do it for. There's no-one there . . .
Fleur (*quietly*) There's me you could not do it for.

But Abe doesn't hear her

Holly You've got to look on the bright side, Abe. No news is good news—I know that doesn't exactly apply, but at least be positive. They got the weekends mixed up. It's easily done.

Fleur searches amongst the jumble-sale things for the bag she wants. We see something black inside, as she takes it to her room

Abe Hasn't anything ever gone wrong in your life?

Holly Of course it has.
Abe What?

Pause

Holly I was left standing at the altar, if you must know.

Pause. Chas refills the cups

Chas Well, that definitely wasn't subtle.
Holly Alcohol's not allowed in this room. It's against the rules.
Chas Yes, I know. Want to go out for a drink?
Holly Cost too much.
Chas It's Saturday night.
Holly I want my own place, Chas. I've scrimped and saved every
    penny I can get my hands on and I'm not going to start spending
    it now.
Chas Spend mine then.
Holly And owe you?
Chas No.
Holly Not even in kind?
Chas You couldn't force me. I'm enjoying my fidelity too much.
Holly I'm enjoying this wine too much.
Chas For what?
Holly For my own good, I think.
Chas (*pouring some more*) Life's a bugger, you know.
Holly Why?
Chas For two reasons. I've worked hard this week. With
    machinery. What I love. I've earned a pay packet and I feel good
    about that. I sent some money home. That's what I came here
    for. But I'm in a strange land with unfamiliar faces, and voices.
    My family, mates are far away. And I miss them. When I was
    there, with them, I hated myself because I wasn't working. No
    self-respect. Life's a bugger.
Holly Was that both reasons?
Chas No.

Pause

Holly I don't get to hear the other one?
Chas Now that you've persuaded me to be faithful, I find that I
    quite fancy you.
Holly Dear God, the man's incorrigible!

Chas But I shall resist all temptations of the flesh, sweet maid of thorns, and stick to breaking the alcohol rules. Drink, Abraham.

Abe It means father of multitudes. But I'm not. I'm not even the father of one now because I've lost her.

They drink

Chas Who?

Abe Janna.

Holly His daughter.

Chas (*whispering*) Has she died?

Abe I don't know. She may have done.

Holly Of course she hasn't. Don't drink any more if you're going to get all maudlin.

Abe Who the hell do you think you are?

Holly What?

Abe You seem to think you have the right to dictate everyone's lives round here.

Holly I don't! They're Ruby's rules . . .

Abe Not the rules of the house, the rules of people's thoughts. Feelings. "What's best for you is this. Look at it this way, don't think that way. What you mean is this, not that. What you do is this, not that . . ."

Holly I just think you're stupid to sit there imagining the worst.

Abe Why can't I imagine what I want to imagine?

Holly That Janna's dead?!

Abe If I want.

Holly Because it's ridiculous. There's bound to be a perfectly simple explanation.

Abe Why should there be? Just because you say so?

Chas Has she been in an accident?

Abe Yes.

Holly No, of course she hasn't.

Abe *How do you know?*

Pause

Holly Abe, you're tired and you haven't slept.

Abe If I prepare myself . . . then it won't be so bad when I hear it, will it?

Fleur comes in wearing a black suit and a small hat with a veil

Holly Fleur, where did you get that?

Fleur In the jumble sale.

Holly It doesn't suit you.

Abe I haven't got a black suit.

Holly You don't need one.

Fleur Elizabeth had a black suit, Abe. Do I look like her?

Abe She must have been to a funeral. She never said where she'd
been. That's why she was so sad. Poor Elizabeth. What if it had
been her daughter's funeral.

Holly Stop it, Abe!

Abe No!! You stop it. Just stop telling me what to do . . .

Abe advances on Holly and Chas gets in the way

Chas Hey, that's enough.

Abe It is. Indeed it is!

Holly He's not going to hurt me. It's all right.

Abe It's not all right and I am going to hurt you.

Chas stops him, though it isn't difficult

Chas What is it with your mouth, Prickles? Won't it stay shut?

Holly I can manage without your help.

Chas Not to keep your mouth shut you can't.

Chas suddenly kisses Holly, much to everyone's amazement

Fleur We could go on a train.

Abe What?

Fleur Now. We could go on a train journey.

*Fleur looks pleadingly at Abe and kisses him. Chas repeats his kiss
on a quietened Holly*

> *Ruby enters. There is a deathly hush. They all part, hide the wine
> bottles and look at Ruby*

Ruby It's my birthday today.

Pause

> I thought you were all out.

Pause

Chas No, we're all in.
Holly Happy birthday, Ruby.

Fleur sings "Happy Birthday To You" and they all join in

Ruby Thank you.

Ruby goes out

Chas rushes the empty wine bottles back to his room

Holly takes the cups out

Fleur Did you like the kiss?
Abe It made me feel better, Fleur. Thank you.
Fleur Do you like me in black?
Abe You're a colourful person really. Like your paintings. Wait there a minute.

Abe goes to his room

Fleur takes off the black hat and jacket and throws on a colourful jumble-sale jumper

Abe comes back in with a child's story book

Abe This was Janna's. I kept it. Would you like me to teach you how to read?

Fleur goes to him delightedly and takes the book

Holly enters

Holly Here's thirty quid and here's my big mouth speaking. Pay your train fare to Colchester. I don't want it back. Go and check things out for yourself.

Abe looks at Fleur who is holding the book

Abe No. They've gone away for the weekend. There's no point in my going.

Abe and Fleur sit down side by side

Chas comes in

Holly pockets most of the money but keeps out a five pound note

Holly OK, Charlie boy. A fiver each in the kitty, and when that's spent, we come home.

Chas I'm staying in.

Holly It's Saturday night!

Chas I'm going to show you some card tricks, Prickles, and we're both going to save our hard-earned.

Ruby enters with a tray of drinks, glasses and three envelopes

They look at her in amazement, then they clear a space on the table

Ruby Would you mind getting my chair, Abraham? The one by the telephone table. Oh, and the telephone table.

Abe goes out

Would you mind pouring the drinks, Charles. Gin and tonic for me.

Holly It's against the r ——

Chas Mouth!

Holly Glass of wine—some more please.

Chas Flower?

Fleur holds up the book showing a page that has a picture of a flower and the word "flower". Chas pours her a drink

Chas Thought you'd be out celebrating.

Ruby Who with?

Chas Friends. Family.

Abe returns with Ruby's chair and the telephone table

Ruby sits in the chair and puts her drink on the telephone table

Ruby I lost them during those ten bad years. People don't like victims, I discovered. You're all victims. Victims of life's warped sense of humour. But I'll drink to you in spite of that.

Fleur And we'll drink to you, Ruby.

Holly To Ruby, who decides when the rules can be broken.

Chas To another week.

Holly Are these your cards? (*She is holding three unopened envelopes*)

Ruby One from my mother. She's in a nursing home. And one from the matron of the nursing home, because my mother asks her to send it.

As Ruby stops Holly looks at the third

Holly And one for Abe.

Abe Me?

Ruby I haven't looked at them.

Holly From Colchester.

Abe leaps to his feet and takes the envelope

Abe It's from Janna. (*He stands holding it*)

Holly Read it, pillock. (*She puts her hand over her mouth*)

Fleur (*gently*) Read it, Abie.

Abe Yes.

Ruby I didn't know, really. I just thought there were two cards on the doormat.

Abe is just standing there

Holly For God's sake, Abe . . .

Abe slits the envelope open. Then he subsides into his chair and slowly pulls out the letter. Fleur sits at his feet. Holly puts her arm round him. The others group as the Lights fade to just the standard lamp

Abe reads the letter out loud

Abe "Hi, Dad! I hope this letter gets to you in plenty of time. I want to change our weekends if that's all right. I wanted to keep it a secret till it actually happened, but I've been accepted for the final auditions for the National Youth Choir, which are this weekend in Manchester. I've already passed two preliminary auditions. I made Mum promise not to tell anyone. Most of all I want you to be proud of me. Dad, guess what? If I make it, I get to go to America! So can I come next weekend instead, and will you keep all your fingers and toes crossed for me? Try and get me that funny little room on the station side of the *Railway Hotel*—the bed's wonderful and the room shakes when the trains go by. I'll be on the usual train on Friday night. If I don't hear from you, I'll assume that's OK. Isn't life wonderful? All my love. Janna."

Happiness spreads amongst them all as they listen. Swelling choir music is heard

The Lights fade to Black-out

CURTAIN

FURNITURE AND PROPERTY LIST

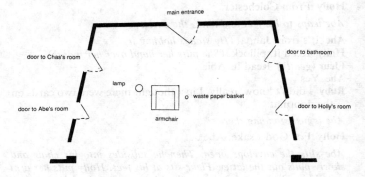

On stage: Winged chair
Standard lamp
Wastepaper bin

Off stage: Small armchair, easel, paints, brushes, half-finished portrait of
Abraham, tall green plant (**Fleur**)
Bunch of flowers, carrier bag. *In it:* bottles of wine (**Chas**)
Towels and wash kits (**Abraham** and **Chas**)
Easy chair (**Abraham**)
Robe (**Fleur**)
Ironing board and iron (**Fleur**)
Ironing (**Abraham**)
Washing-up bowl (**Holly**)
Table (**Fleur**)
Kettle (**Holly**)
Easy chair, ironing (**Chas**)
Carrier bags. *In them:* jumble sale clothes and a chipped vase
(**Fleur** and **Holly**)
Suitcase and a wrapped parcel (**Abraham**)
Kettle (**Fleur**)
Bottles of wine (**Chas**)
Four white tea cups (**Holly**)

Child's story book **(Abraham)**
Money, including a five pound note **(Holly)**
Tray. *On it:* drinks, glasses, three letters **(Ruby)**
Chair and telephone table **(Abraham)**

Personal: **Abraham:** box containing letters
Chas: coin
Abraham: rent money
Holly: rent money
Chas: pocket knife incorporating corkscrew

LIGHTING PLOT

Practical fittings required: standard lamp

Interior. The same scene throughout

To open: The standard lamp, covering spot

Cue 1	**Abraham** puts the letter back in the box *Lights come up*	(Page 1)
Cue 2	**Ruby** switches off the standard lamp *Black-out*	(Page 14)
Cue 3	**Ruby** goes out in the Black-out *Pause; then bring up lighting*	(Page 14)
Cue 4	The others group *Fade to practical with covering spot*	(Page 25)
Cue 5	Choir music *Lights fade to Black-out*	(Page 25)

EFFECTS PLOT

Cue 1 **Abraham** reads his letter   (Page 1)
        Voice-over of child reading letter

Cue 2 **Abe:** "'All my love. Janna'."   (Page 25)
        Bring up choir music

MADE AND PRINTED IN GREAT BRITAIN BY
LATIMER TREND & COMPANY LTD PLYMOUTH

MADE IN ENGLAND